Farm to Table for Schools

Chef Budd Cohen

© 2014 by Chef Budd Cohen

All rights reserved worldwide. No part of this publication may be transmitted or copied in any form or by any means, electronic, mechanical, photocopying, recording, or otherwise without the prior written permission of the publisher.

This publication is designed to provide general information regarding the subject matter covered. In the event you use any of the information in this book for yourself, the author and publisher assume no responsibility for your actions.

ISBN-13: 978-1502489777

ISBN-10: 1502489775

First Printing, 2014

Printed in the United States of America

Photo Credit for Author Photo: Michael Branscom

Farm to Table for Schools

Dedication

To my wife, Stacey, and my children, Alex and Abby, with appreciation for their love and support and their willingness to accompany me on this journey. To my mom, Joan, for her support, and to my late father, Lewis, who would be very proud.

Table of Contents

Foreword _____ 9

Introduction _____ 13

5 Motivating Points _____ 17

The Intersection of My Personal History and the Background of the Movement _____ 25

When Farm to Table Came on My Radar _____ 37

9 Areas of Focus_____ 51

Steps to Bring Farm to Table to Your Environment _____ 75

Conclusion _____ 97

About the Author _____ 101

Foreword

by Dr. Timothy Lynch

No childhood is complete without the memory of the cafeteria lunch lady. She was the underappreciated, and often feared, deliverer of a lunch of largely unknown origin. It wasn't her fault that you suffered through five days of government cheese and hockey puck burgers. The school food supply chain has relied on heavily preserved food products for the purpose of long term storage and limited preparation costs. Now, there is a new approach to the school cafeteria food supply chain - the "Farm to School" (F2S) philosophy. Spearheading this new food philosophy is Chef Budd Cohen.

Chef Budd Cohen has dedicated his culinary career to promoting the connection between local farms and the cafeteria. His culinary ingenuity and ability to build relationships with farmers is transforming the culinary landscape in schools. In this book, Chef Budd uses his culinary journey to instruct other chefs, food service directors, administrators and all interested parties about how to alter their culinary journey, rerouting them to the local farm community.

This book fills a void in the culinary arts by outlining, in detail, the steps necessary to connect your school to a network of local farmers and farm cooperatives that will supply you with farm fresh produce and meats to introduce new tastes, fresh ingredients, and higher nutritional value to your school meals.

Chef Budd's enthusiasm, cheerful personality, and motivational approach to the Farm to School movement have transformed many schools across Pennsylvania and Delaware. In this book, he has designed and perfected the instruction manual for a cafeteria conversion to healthier farm-sourced ingredients, while supporting your local community and economy.

Dr. Timothy Lynch is a Science Teacher at William Penn Charter School and a Researcher at the University of Pennsylvania

Introduction

Why write this book?

After years of learning about and experiencing first-hand the farm to table movement, I felt compelled to share what I have learned along the way. My hope is that this book will be a guide to help you serve more local, healthful food at your school and to help create a more environmentally sustainable planet.

The farm to table movement (F2T) and farm to school movement (F2S) are connected in many ways. Farm to table could be considered the larger entity that encompasses all farm direct food distribution settings, with the recipients being groups and individuals. Under this umbrella are many sub-categories. Some of these categories can be broken down even further into sub-groups. A good example of this could be farm to pre-school (F2PS), a sub-group of farm to school. Whether you are involved in an educational setting that is privately run or are in a publicly operated institution, this information should be valuable. It is not difficult to serve local food in your establishment, but it will take patience, planning and communication.

The collection of stories, points and steps compiled in this book will help you learn how to effectively plan, communicate, and execute a farm to school program.

Who is This Book For?

This book is geared towards several people. Chefs, students, teachers, food service directors, school administrators, facility managers, and business leaders. All can benefit from reading this book.

There are many ways that establishments can benefit from serving local foods and supporting local agriculture. In addition to showing you how to support local agriculture, this guide will demonstrate how your institution can be more sustainable in other areas as well.

What Can You Get Out of This Book?

Chapter one walks through five top reasons for adopting the farm to table concept in your institution. Chapters two and three document my background and history. Chapter four lays out nine general points of focus for sustainability and chapter five outlines the steps you need to take to install a farm to school program at your institution.

It is important to do some self-reflection before attempting to embark on this project. Eating is a personal act. This book can be thought of as a starting point. Consider it a compass that will point you in the right direction. There is no cookie cutter model for taking farm to table into an establishment. Each situation and institution should be handled in a unique way.

Determine your goals and motivation. As you move through the chapters, ask yourself why you are considering embarking on this journey. Evaluate as you go as to where you are at in your own mind with the project. Farm to table can be a complicated process, so you need to understand where you are coming from and what your reasons are for pursuing it.

The main goals of this publication are to inspire and educate. In a nutshell, this book may inspire you and show you how to take the next step. I will list successes and learning moments. The goal is to educate you and encourage you to move beyond what has been done.

Local produce at school farm stand

Chapter 1:
5 Motivating Points

Outlined here are five of the motivating factors that many people may experience in this process. Each motivating factor could stand alone as your only motivation. These motivating factors will vary in importance from one individual to the next, but they are all tied together. An example of this could be the idealistic theory of saving the world compared to the idea of making a stronger financial statement for your company or school. These two motivations are very different from each other and could be on some levels considered opposing thoughts. But with compromise and flexibility, all these motivations can work together.

This compromise works for F2T programs all the time. For example, two obviously different motivations are working at my school right now. I am writing this part of the book at the time of year in Pennsylvania when the summer harvest is in full swing. It is early in September. Schools in the area are starting a new academic year. Last week, I went to order supplies for the upcoming week. I did some comparative shopping and found that I could purchase tomatoes farm direct and have them delivered to my door for less cost and get a much better product than if I ordered tomatoes from my "broad line distributor." By purchasing the ripe, tasty, farm direct in season tomatoes, we are able to achieve several goals. My goals of wanting a more sustainable planet (environmental stewardship) and serving tastier, more nutritious products were accomplished. Some motivation is to take a step toward making positive financial results for the contracting company I work for (capital gains improvement), and that goal was accomplished as well.

As we go through the five motivating factors, please keep in mind that it is personal. There are no wrong answers. The modern/current F2T movement is so young that we cannot say what will happen to it. Go with whatever motivates you.

Motivation #1: Save the World

There are some who use science to think about the impact of the human race's carbon footprint on the earth. Others view stewardship with a more idealistic thought process that considers the ethical treatment of people and animals. Both groups may be trying to get to the same result; that is, making our world a place where we can thrive for many years to come.

Environmental sustainability is a big motivating factor. Buying local, sustainably produced goods can have a large impact on the future. "Act locally – think globally" is an often-heard phrase. Starting and maintaining a farm to table program at your institution can have a huge impact on our future. That is a great example of how a small step can impact the larger picture.

Motivation #2: Strive to Promote Good Health

The second reason is that more sustainably produced, farm direct products can help lead to better health. A plant begins to decay and lose nutrients as soon as it is picked. By serving local produce and supporting local agriculture, you can help to encourage healthy eating for you, your family and the larger community. Plus, the more locally produced goods that are bought and sold, the greater the demand and, consequently, the greater production of those goods, theoretically lowering the prices and increasing availability. Buy more local goods and more local goods will become available at lower costs.

As farmers use fewer poisonous pesticides and herbicides, they will have less of a negative impact on the environment and the people who live in the community where the food is grown. In addition, sustainable and organic agricultural practices can be less risky for the farmers, their families, and farm workers as a result of using decreasing amounts of harsh chemicals.

Motivation #3: Eat Naturally Tastier Food

This is an excellent reason to subscribe to the farm to table concept because people want to eat tastier food. There is no comparison between the taste of a tomato that is grown fresh, local and in season and a tomato that is commercially produced through industrial agriculture. In season, local foods taste much better than foods that have traveled long distances. It is sometimes difficult to describe the way real, whole food tastes in comparison to imitation or artificial flavors to someone who is not used to eating them. By artificial or imitation flavors, I am referring to highly processed foods that contain a lot of flavor enhancing chemicals and/or fat, sugar and salt. To get people to eat more fresh fruit and vegetables, you should strive to serve the best and tastiest produce that you can procure.

Motivation #4: Go Greener for Cultural Reasons

Your institution may want to be greener for cultural reasons. For example, if the history of the institution is rooted in agriculture, there could be a desire to retain that part of the history. Recently, I met a gentleman who worked with Whole Foods when the company was just starting out. He told me a story about one of the store openings and how the owners engaged someone to bless and purify the site. This story is an example of how Whole Foods executives wanted the culture of their company to be. There are many companies that truly want to go greener.

Marketing is one of the reasons a company may want to be greener and it can be used in a positive or negative way. There are some institutions that "fake" going green with smoke and mirrors just to pay lip service to going green without actually incorporating those practices. I have noticed instances where broad line distributors have used insignias next to products that are produced geographically close to the distributor.

That is good marketing and saves some fossil fuel and I can see how the reasons for doing it make sense to them; however, that is not going green in my opinion, and it seems more like marketing than sustainability. I give them credit for taking a step in the right direction, but it will be wonderful if and when they move further toward serving more sustainable products. In most cases, it doesn't seem like these companies source anything differently. They just put an insignia next to the products' descriptions. If you look at the bacon at my local distributor, for example, you will find a product that is made locally. I don't have anything against this product; it is very tasty. I have driven by the plant many times. It is an industrial pork product-producing factory. The problem, however, is that there is no way of knowing how the animals are treated at such a facility. We don't know where the swine are trucked in from. How much of our food dollars are actually going to the farmer? How are the workers in that plant treated?

Motivation #5: Increase Profitability or Reduce the Subsidy of Your Food Service Program

The fifth reason to use the farm to table model is to increase profit or financial stability. If done the right way, serving healthier food, increasing sustainability, and taking care of people ethically can lead to more profit. You must always look at the cost and the return of your food purchases. When you can balance sales of higher profit items with sales of lower profit items, you can make a menu that works for you financially. If you are locked into a pricing structure with your current offerings, you can often introduce new items and price them accordingly. In today's business climate, sustainability or stewardship can lead in many ways to a strong, positive financial picture.

Chapter 2: The Intersection of My Personal History and the Background of the Movement

Hanging around with my grandfather, Walter Lengle, was always an exciting adventure. He somehow got the nickname Pomp-Pomp, which I think originated from my cousin, Cesta. Cesta recently told me stories about the times she and Pomp went foraging for dandelions and shared farm tour adventures. When I was with Pomp, we would often go to local farms to get produce, eggs or whatever was available at the time. Pomp had a house in Fleetwood, Pennsylvania, and he was part owner of a farm nearby.

Along with my grandmother Katherine, my grandfather canned many fruits and vegetables throughout the year and had a large supply saved for the winter. Many of their dishes had deep roots in the agriculture of Pennsylvania from the 1940s through the 1980s. A room in the basement was stocked with their home preserved products, filling several walls. My grandparents also had a large garden where they grew many of the products they canned.

When we took trips to local farms, Pomp would speak Pennsylvania Dutch, a dialect that comes from German and is often heard in this area. At some of the farms, we picked strawberries, and at others, we gathered eggs from the henhouse or just visited to see what was going on. I certainly had no idea how these experiences would affect me later in life. Looking back, I wish I had paid more attention to what was going on around me.

My grandfather also used to take me foraging for wild nuts. I believe they were either chestnuts or walnuts. He had certain stops along the way and knew the best time of year to find them. In *Omnivore's Dilemma*, the author describes a meal that was comprised of ingredients foraged from the local environment. This reminded me of my grandfather. Foraging is the oldest known way humans fed themselves. Foraged foods are not grown by humans and do not leave a manmade carbon footprint. During the time when Pomp was growing up and when I knew him, industrial food really was not as prevalent as it is today. But in his later life, processed foods became more common and the culture my grandfather lived in was quickly disappearing.

Growing up, we always had farm fresh eggs. Today, my mom has a friend named Peggy who has chickens. When we go to visit, she always has the best eggs. The eggs Peggy's chickens produce are varied in appearance depending on the variety of chicken they came from. Sometimes we get blue or green, brown, white or even speckled eggs. The chickens are for the most part free range and eat lots of grubs and other insects. The varied diet and the fresh air and exercise help produce eggs that are highly nutritious and have a deep yellow/orange yolk.

My parents and grandparents made connections with local orchards. Frecon Orchards in Boyertown, PA is a family-run business that has found its way from humble roots in the past. Several years ago, on a farm tour with James DeMarsh, who was the manager of Common Market at the time, we visited Frecon. With our host, Mr. Frecon, we journeyed in his old pickup truck to the top of the orchard and saw a tremendous crop of peaches, nectarines, apples and pears. He explained how they are working with Penn State University's agriculture department to develop new varieties of tree fruit and are developing new integrated pest management (IPM) techniques. Tree fruit (particularly stone fruit) is a difficult product to grow without the use of chemicals, and pest pressure on orchard fruit is heavy. Frecon Orchards uses a variety of old and new farming practices. One such technique was burning down the brush around the fruit trees. I learned that if the brush is lower, the bugs are less likely to jump up on the fruit. Physical removal of the brush cuts down the amount of chemicals they need to use.

Frecon Orchard visit

Another answer to the question of how to cut back on inorganic chemical use is by employing positive influencing insects. I am no expert on the subject of IPM, but the way I would describe the use of good bugs is that farms set traps that capture insects to see how many and what kinds are present. When they see the kinds of bad bugs that destroy fruit crops in large numbers, they attempt to kill only those bugs. Mr. Frecon described a system that includes releasing good bugs that combat the bad bugs at the peak of their presence. Another way this can work is when trapped bad bugs are procreating, farmers can release natural chemicals (pheromones) that inhibit the breeding of only the bad insects that are hurting the crops.

Another very successful local farmer, Curt Fifer, who owns Fifer Orchards, compares the new IPM methods to those of a smart bomb. A smart bomb only aims for a very specific target, just like current pest control methods only go after specific targeted pests. At Circle M Orchard in New Jersey, the owner and his son are testing what I would describe as a twisty tie that is attached to the limb of the tree, which releases a chemical that specifically targets a certain pest. Circle M and Fifer are both working with the University of Delaware on these new agriculture projects.

My mother is a huge fan of New Jersey blueberries. Each year, she made arrangements with a farmer in south Jersey to get blueberries. She waited until the peak of blueberry season to get the biggest, sweetest berries. She would call the farm and order many pounds at a time and my dad would drive down and pick them up. Once home, Mom would sort, wash, dry and freeze the berries.

When I was growing up in Reading, there were fewer processed foods. Refrigeration only became widely available in the United States in households in the 1940's and 1950's. Processing became more prevalent as well. When I was born in the 1960's, there were still very limited processed foods. This caused people to have to cook foods from scratch, and grocery stores at the time carried a larger supply of whole foods. Processed foods became popular as soon as they were introduced.

One philosophy I go by today is that if there is an ingredient listed on a label that your great grandmother would not have recognized as food, that is probably not good for me. That philosophy can also be found in Michael Pollan's book, *Food Rules.*

In the 1960's and 1970's, meal preparation changed from scratch cooking to convenience cooking. More women went to work and did not have as much time to cook. Many more households became environments with two working adults. Preparing food from scratch is something that every homemaker and chef used to do, but not anymore, both in our schools and at home. Processed foods that taste good and are cost effective are readily available, so institutions use them often. Another thought I have heard and fully agree with is that it has come to a point in the food service industry when institutional feeding is more about using a box cutter to open up processed foods than actually using a chef's knife or a vegetable peeler.

When an institution or household or anyone for that matter decides to revert to scratch cooking, they have to retrain themselves and make time for food preparation, such as peeling, dicing, chopping, etc. It is sometimes difficult to teach a food service staff that may run a school cafeteria to prep food again from scratch. Perhaps they never even learned how to make items that are not already processed. When attempting to do this project, do not be discouraged by the lack of training and enthusiasm towards these new processes. In the end, the cooks or chefs will create a much better product, a product that they can stand behind and be proud of.

When I graduated high school in 1982, I had no idea that food and agriculture would be a huge part of my life.

After one year at Widener University, I decided that college was not for me and I started working. During the summer after my first year of college, I moved with several friends to Long Beach Island (LBI) in New Jersey to work and enjoy the summer at the beach. I got my next taste of food services that summer working at two establishments. The first was a Greek restaurant called the Greek Gourmet. My other job was stocking a local bar with beer in the mornings. It was an LBI traditional bar called Nardis. I found out very quickly that working two jobs did not leave much time for play, and I moved home before the end of the summer.

The next fall, I moved to Delaware and I found a job at The Royal Exchange. I found it difficult to make ends meet comfortably, so I moved back home after about a year.

Next, I worked for Stephen Bonner at Boscov's Department Store in Reading. Working with Stephen was incredible, as I learned so much and really fell in love with catering and food as an art. In 1988, I married Stacey and we moved to Baltimore so I could attend culinary school. From 1988-1990, I got serious about my career and about food. I still had no idea during those years how industrial agriculture and being a chef were tied together.

From a chef's perspective, my passion for good food has always been the reason why I am in this industry. I am very enthusiastic about food in general and I have learned to share my enthusiasm with others. The term "foodie" is certainly applicable to me. Today, with so many TV shows, Internet sites, blogs and global communication based on food, the bar has been raised. People know good food and are increasingly more open to food as art in both modern and traditional ways.

While in Baltimore, I worked at several locations and gained new skills in food production and management. I received two degrees from Baltimore Culinary College. Baltimore was fun, but we wanted to move closer to Philadelphia and home where we could start a family.

We moved back to the area and found an apartment in Roxborough, a neighborhood of Philly. I got a job at a famous Philadelphia restaurant called The Commissary, where I worked for the owner, Steven Poses, and his partners until the restaurant closed. I worked my way up to executive chef in my short time there and learned many new recipes and techniques. I learned about Thai, Southwestern, traditional Jewish Food dishes, Italian, Cajun, French and many other ethnic cuisines.

When The Commissary closed, I moved to the Sheraton Plaza in Valley Forge, PA and became the executive chef of the hotel. I was hired by Klaus Biber, who has been, and still is, an inspiration, great friend and mentor to me. Chef Klaus taught me how to run a hotel food service operation and instilled in me a commitment to a coaching/counseling management style. I applied at IKEA to run the food services at the Plymouth Meeting, PA store, and they called me and offered me the position. They offered training in customer relations, and we learned about Nordic cuisine. IKEA brought in chefs from Sweden and Norway to train their managers and chefs.

After working at IKEA, a friend asked me if I would help cook at a company called Chilton Publishing in Radnor, PA. He worked for a new locally owned food service Contract Company called Williamson Hospitality. Roger Kelly was one of their regional managers who helped me a lot at Chilton. I became the chef first, but quickly moved to the manager position. I asked Chef Klaus if he would like to come cook with me.

In less than a year, another manager approached and said he was leaving the company and that my taking over the account he was leaving, William Penn Charter School, could be a good idea. I asked the owners if I could transfer to Penn Charter and they made me an offer. This proved to be a pivotal step in my career, because it was at Penn Charter that I became acquainted with F2S.

Chapter 3: When Farm to Table Came on My Radar

Over the next 15 years, I ran K-12 grade school food-service operations, 12 years at Penn Charter followed by three years at Sanford School in Delaware. During my time at Penn Charter, Williamson Hospitality was bought by CulinArt, a National Food Service Company from New York.

Soon after I moved from Chilton Publishing, Chef Klaus joined me once again. About the same time, I met Terry DiPaul, who became my assistant manager and handled many of the office/administrative duties. Terry, Klaus and I made up the management team.

In 2006, I returned to Penn Charter after summer break and it really started to bother me that the tomatoes I was planning on serving to the Board of Trustees were not at all the quality I had been eating all summer. Great tomatoes, some heirloom, all local, were readily available from my friend, farmer Barry Davis, and his wife Peggy. I decided to buy and serve their tomatoes, peppers and cucumbers, and whatever I could get in season, instead of the produce I could get from my large purveyors. The critical product was the tomato. I love summer fresh ripe tomatoes, and I have even been known to eat them like apples.

Visit to Barry and Peg Davis' farm stand

After that, I started regularly bringing in vanloads of product to school from Barry. Folks immediately appreciated the quality and the value of the farm fresh, in season goods. After that Penn Charter board luncheon, one of the board members asked me if I had ever heard of a book called *The Omnivore's Dilemma*, and he highly recommended it. I bought and read it, and quite honestly, the author, Michael Pollan, is a genius. That book changed my life. I highly recommend that everyone read it, especially people interested in the food industry. The understanding of where our food comes from and how it gets to our plates has led me to crusade for the farm to table movement. As Pollan states, "What we eat has tremendous impact on how we are going to leave this world for future generations." Lynne White, Jr., *Dynamo and Virgin Reconsidered: Essays in the Dynamism of Western Culture* (Cambridge: MIT Press, 1968), 60–1. The book also opened my eyes to the industrial food chain, of which I was a part for many years. It reconnected me in many ways to the soil and the sun, and how the natural systems of poly-culture agriculture work. *The Omnivore's Di-*

lemma prepared me to take it to the next level. I now was in a position to feed local foods to the masses, I knew why it was important and I worked for a company and a school that allowed me to do it.

Over the years, at Penn Charter I learned about Quakerism and realized that the farm to table movement fit with Quaker values and my own personal values as well. I found that Penn Charter was a perfect place to educate people about the value of farm to school projects. I began incorporating F2S lessons in my afterschool and summer cooking classes. But there wasn't a way to get these products delivered, farm direct in large quantities, on account, to my school. Common Market and Lancaster Farm Fresh Co-Op (two farm to institution distributors) were not available to me yet. About that time, I began to realize that it is very important to educate students about what they are eating because they are the ones who can turn the system back around to a more sustainable food chain. I also wanted them to lead healthier lives, so I often promoted nutrition tied with F2S programs.

I was invited to a farm to school summit hosted by a division of White Dog Enterprises. At the meeting, there were great guest speakers from schools that were doing F2S on a large scale. One of the main reasons we all met was to discuss a farm to table distribution system. The Idea was called "Common Market," and it was to be a not-for-profit farm to institution distribution system. Common Market just celebrated the completion of five years of being in operation.

A huge issue farm to institution programs faced at the time was distribution. My good friend David Green, his boss, Porter Bush, and some other local CulinArt folks were also in attendance. CulinArt at George School, directed by our manager, Joe Ducati, was also doing farm to table, and CulinArt had invested in a local farm. Tom Eich, our corporate president, Joe Pacifico, the owner, and Mike Purcell, vice president from CulinArt, continue to support sustainability programs and are advocates for supporting local producers. On a local level, Dan McGill, the president of my division, is a F2S advocate as well. When Dan took over our division, I was working on bringing local dairy to Penn Charter.

Dan and I visited Merrymead Farm in Lansdale, PA, and we made a deal to have milk delivered to Penn Charter directly from the farm. Making this deal happen was not easy. I had to persuade all three parties involved -- my company, the school and the farmer -- that this could and would work out. Finally, the industry was starting to change.

Dan McGill visiting Merrymead

Working at Penn Charter, I was making great connections and forming relationships with people interested in moving environmental stewardship further. The Head of School, Dr. Earl Ball, and his successor, Dr. Darryl Ford, both support the F2S movement. I have found that science teachers, for obvious reasons, are often more involved with agriculture projects and are often committed to promoting environmental sustainability. Dr. Timothy Lynch, who was then chair of the Science department at Penn Charter, was and is still a great source of inspiration and information.

Common Market came to fruition in 2008 and I have been told that Penn Charter was the first school to which the Common Market ever delivered. They were located only a few blocks from each other. Now, I could get farm direct goods through a not-for-profit distribution system. Two people, Tatiana Garcia-Granados and Haile Johnston, are the masterminds behind Common Market and the most instrumental in making it a reality. They had the vision and are still taking it to the next level today. Common Market is an operation that is a model for other cities in our country to follow. By the time I left Penn Charter in 2009 to take on my next project, they had all the systems in place to carry on the F2S tradition.

In the summer of 2009, CulinArt offered me a new challenge. I was offered and accepted the position of food service director at the Sanford School in Hockessin, Delaware.

The culture and history of Sanford was steeped in agriculture. The grounds it stands on were once a 100+ acre farm. The faculty, staff and students raised most of their own food. The business manager, Becky McCudden, is great to work with and is an advocate for the farm to school movement. The head of school, Mark Anderson, was also very supportive and great to work with. It makes all the difference for a school foodservice account when the client, administration and faculty are enthusiastic about sustainability.

At the time, Lancaster Farm Fresh Co-op was running deliveries in that area and I began working more with them on a weekly basis. Lancaster Farm Fresh Co-op is a group of farmers in Lancaster, PA, who produce lots of organic products and deliver to institutions covering a large geographic area. I met Casey Spacht, the general manager, for the first time many years before, and we had worked together while I was at Penn Charter.

While working at Sanford School, there was an agreement being worked out with the Department of Agriculture, the Governor's office, the Department of Education and the school districts to bring local products into the schools. I was invited to Dover and met Governor Jack Markel and Ed Kee, the Secretary of Agriculture. The meeting in Dover was a summit for the school districts to meet the local farms and learn all about F2S. We were already doing F2S at Sanford School.

Meeting Secretary Kee was an honor. He helped Sanford School get to the next level of F2T projects. The first time we met, I asked him, "Secretary Kee, would you come to Sanford School sometime and speak about agriculture and farming?" He leaned over and said, "Sure, I will visit Sanford, and call me Ed." I got Ed's contact information and over the next few months we made plans to host an Earth Day celebration, featuring Ed as the guest speaker, and then an "Eco-Village" type fair afterward. The whole event went great, and for the first time, I felt like I had moved from an advocate in my account to a leader of sustainability for the region.

The school started a gardening project, we ran lots of farm tours, and we planted the start of a new apple/peach orchard. In the kitchen, we were making many items from scratch and had begun composting with a local industrial composter. Between composting and recycling, we were practically a zero-waste "landfill" kitchen operation. For paper goods, we purchased compostable products, and we installed a new washing machine for more effective dishware washing. Two of my key people at the time, Ken Szaroleta and Chef Mike Galvin, were instrumental in our composting operation. When we started composting, they even took food scraps home and composted them at their sites.

That summer, David Green and I attended the National Farm to School Network Conference in Burlington, VT. The conference in Vermont offered the chance to make national contacts and opened my eyes to what was going on in the movement nationwide. It was attended by folks doing F2S in all 50 states. Three congressmen/women came to speak to the group, the USDA hosted many seminars, and it was four days of celebrating the movement.

What came naturally to me, due to my history and circumstances, was going on all over the country. Feeding nutritious food to children is now a national goal, with President Barack Obama being an advocate. First Lady Michelle Obama led a tremendous crusade for healthy foods for kids. At the conference, a chef from the White House addressed the attendees via a recorded message.

In 2013, I was offered the opportunity to run the food services at Philadelphia College of Osteopathic Medicine (PCOM) on City Avenue in Philadelphia, and I accepted the position. This was my fourth account with Williamson/CulinArt in my 17 years with them.

Sanford School was poised to truly take it to the next level of sustainability, so six months ago, I fully took the reins of PCOM, and I am blessed once again to have the opportunity to bring my F2S techniques and programs to another institution. For a third time, my client, and the president, Dr. Matthew Shure, are supportive of my F2S program. PCOM is a great learning institution, and in general, the faculty, staff and students want to eat healthy. Again, I have found like-minded partners in my chef, Steve Baumann, my assistant manager, Judy Gammons, and my catering production chef, Janice Callahan. We have formed a core team at PCOM that focuses on scratch cooking, quality ingredients and serving tasty nutritional foods. No matter where you are starting, there will always be a next step.

The balancing act is ongoing and varies depending on the situation. Some of the tough questions that arise are: How much processed food is okay? How do you balance costs in today's economy? How do you produce massive quantities of local nutritious foods that all people can afford? How do you convince people that this is the right thing to do?

We are surrounded by palatable foods more than ever. Generations before us spent much more time during the day getting food and preparing it for their families. I like to look at cooking as a team sport. Involving the children in the kitchen at a young age can be rewarding. Children are more likely to eat something they helped prepare. Today, diabetes, high blood pressure and obesity are at epidemic proportions in America, due in part to the processed foods we eat. If we eat foods we prepare from scratch, we can control what goes into our dishes and what kind of food goes into our bodies. This was not a problem seventy-five or 100 years ago. Processed foods were not available. People spent a longer time every day at home cooking. What meals can you cook from scratch in a half an hour?

You may be wondering: how does this affect the food services at my child's school? Or if you work at a school, how does this affect you? First of all, your school cafeteria could offer more whole foods, whole grains or leaner proteins. That is a good start. We are eating at our schools and businesses more than ever, so it feels like it is even more important to eat healthier at those places. Farm to institution projects lead to healthier eating.

Chapter 4:
9 Areas of Focus

This section of the book identifies nine areas of focus that will act as a framework to guide you toward your goals. Some areas of focus can be applied specifically to farm to table activities, while other areas are broader in a way that could complement your program. In most of the nine points, there are personal motivation concepts. Readers, nonetheless, should learn about the complex issues associated with industrial farming and the food service industry and how that relates to school food service programs. These areas of focus are also meant to keep you fresh and on point. People are interested in sustainability on many different levels, so you will want to take each point and evaluate how you may want to use it.

Area of Focus #1: Create Quality Partnerships

The best way to learn about the most current information and techniques is to visit farmers and producers, and the easiest way to meet farmers is to attend farmers markets or farm stands. My two favorite farmers markets in this area are the Phoenixville Market on Saturdays and the Leesport Market on Wednesdays. One of the best things about farmers markets is that the producers are often on hand and are thrilled to chat with you about products, production methods, current seasonal events and harvests. Respect their time. You may have to wait a bit if they are already engaged in a conversation or are otherwise busy. I have seen farm to table marketing that states, "Know the people that grow your food" and "Don't buy food from strangers." I fully agree with these statements.

Establish partnerships with area restaurants, organizations, and institutions. Lots of people in all walks of life are doing farm to table. People who are engaged in farm to table activities often are willing to share best practices, vendor referrals and product availability information. In turn, feel free to share information with these folks as well. Your enthusiasm will be contagious. Don't be afraid to make new contacts. If you have the opportunity to operate in several states or nationwide, there are organizations in each state. Examples in my state include: the Pennsylvania Association for Sustainable Agriculture (PASA) and the Pennsylvania Department of Agriculture. Nationwide, there are many groups that can help as well. Organizations such as the United States Department of Agriculture (USDA), Farm Aid, and the National Farm to School Network are a few with which you can start.

Partner with your consumers. Promote farm to table in your environment and see how your students/employees/customers react. In school settings, the teachers and students will give you feedback on new products and new dishes. Listen to feedback, track sales, and offer educational and promotional marketing and activities. Try to look at criticism as constructive feedback. People take food very personally, and you cannot please everyone's palate. I have found middle school and older lower school students to be a little more open to these concepts and foods. Try not to allow negative comments about new foods that are seasonal and special. For example, I find Brussels sprouts to be delicious. They are particularly tasty when picked fresh, and a stalk of Brussels sprouts makes an attractive display. Some children and adults may express a distaste for them, but encourage them to at least give them a try. Remember you cannot win every battle.

In higher education settings, some students are very interested in eating healthy and appreciate local, sustainable foods. I have found that buying locally available items that most consumers are not familiar with can actually spark good conversations. For example, I recently used local dandelion, tatsoi, lacanodo kale, bitter melon, stinging nettles, purple tomatillos and cape gooseberries (ground cherries). I make an informational sign and put out a sample of the product. By starting conversations with the people we feed and by explaining your interest in the farm to table movement to them, we are joining in a partnership with our end users. For me, the partnership with my customers and students is entered into when they enjoy some local products that we have introduced.

Promote quality partnerships within your organization. The most helpful, effective way to make a farm to table program work is by engaging people on the work food chain who have an interest in the subject. Your boss, clients, employees and administrators, board members and others can all have a critical impact on how far you take your program. Take people on farm tours and engage them in conversation. If you directly run a foodservice kitchen, you will need support from your cooks and prep people. If you are in a corporate foodservice situation, you need buy-in from your district food service manager and his or her boss.

It is critical that you partner with some distributors. In many areas of the country, there are farmer co-ops and not-for-profit groups that will distribute goods to you from many farmers all at once. Most purveyors can also be helpful, but be aware of how they are getting the food and how many middlemen there are between you and the farmers. Folks like Larry Tambone, with Ambrosia Foods, have been working with farmers in our area for years and are happy to supply locally produced products.

Area of Focus #2: Support Sustainable Local Agriculture

Support sustainable local agriculture by purchasing goods that you can easily trace back to the source. If organic local products are available at prices you can afford, that is best. Develop a repertoire of questions to ask farmers, producers and distributors. If you are not sure how an item was grown or what the farmer is adding to the crops (e.g., pesticides), just ask. Be thoughtful and not condescending, and try to set up these meetings ahead of time. Don't be too picky about the grade of the product all of the time. I have often bought No. 2 grade products from farmers. Not all peppers, for example, can be perfect. We must learn to work around the dings and bruises that come with growing produce. Usually, these items are sold at a lower price and can work perfectly for production. Some estimates state that as much as 30% of our food goes to waste, and in many cases it is unnecessary.

Buy everything you can to try and increase your usage of local sustainable products. For example, you may find that there are many foods like dried beans, flour, frozen meats, cheeses, eggs, jams, honey, preserves and yogurt that are available from local farms year round. Some of these may be out of your comfort zone as far as production or prices are concerned, but do the best you can. Meats from local, sustainable producers, for example, can be costly. You can get around this by buying meats that can be used in dishes that feature non-protein items like pasta, grains and vegetables, such as bison chili, which is on my menu this week along with a soup featuring smoked ham hocks. List the names of the farms or locations on the menu to get the most for your purchasing dollar.

When you meet with farmers and producers face-to-face, be prepared to pay full price for their products. Don't try to beat them up for deals. Remember, you are trying to support them. I have found that when you buy a lot and show them that you are on their side, they will sometimes throw in a little more or offer you a price break on their own. Don't forget, the object is to support sustainable local agriculture.

Area of Focus #3: Encourage Others Around You to Become Leaders

Encourage others around you to become leaders and advocates for change. We need support from others in this effort with the hope that they will eventually take it upon themselves. In school settings, this is more easily done because clubs and groups that focus on sustainability may already exist on your campus. These groups may provide people who could become leaders in the movement and help promote change. When it comes to the administration and board of trustees, reach out to individuals who can go on to support you and others in the cause.

Listen to people and find out where they are coming from. They may be interested in growing the sustainability program in ways you may not have imagined. Empower and encourage them to take the next step. Some people are natural leaders, and they could be assets to the farm to table movement.

Share your enthusiasm with everyone. You will find that there are interested people everywhere. Display your local products, offer tastings, and don't be afraid to put yourself out there. You will find that some people will respond very positively, and they may go on to influence others.

Stick with the program. Providing nutritious food is the right thing to do. Success can come easily in developing a good farm to institution program. Keep in mind that you are doing the right thing and lead by example because the chances are good that others will follow your lead.

When you are out there developing leaders, you must remember the successes and not dwell on the situations that didn't work out perfectly. Everything is a learning experience and without some failures, you will not evolve. Don't let your potential leaders around you see negativity or disappointment; instead, show them that you can learn as well. Developing other leaders within your organization will ensure that there will be others who will continue the work after you move on.

Area of Focus #4: Reduce Your Carbon Footprint

Reducing your carbon footprint in your institution goes hand-in-hand with a farm to table program, and it only takes small changes to put your institution on the right track. Kitchens, cafeterias, dining areas and preparation areas can reduce their use of fossil fuels by turning off equipment, lights and refrigerators when not in use and by switching to more sustainable wind, water or solar energy.

You can reduce the waste stream produced in your food service areas as well. Deep fryer oil can be converted into bio-diesel fuel, and local companies in some areas of our country will pay you for your waste oil.

Composting kitchen and cafeteria waste is another good way to reduce the amount of waste coming from your foodservice program. There are many companies that will do this for you for a fee or you can do it yourself. It may be difficult in some settings to do the large scale composting that an institutional kitchen would require, but in some urban areas, there are companies that are able to handle large quantities. Coffee grounds can be offered to your guests as a good source of material needed to do proper composting. The best book I have found on the subject of composting is *The Rodale book of Composting*.

Obviously, a good recycling program for glass, metal, plastic, paper and cardboard is in order, but not always easily done. In addition, your café may have the capabilities to use china and glass for service, in which case there are more options to reduce your carbon footprint. If your facility cannot handle the use of non-disposable service ware, there are a growing number of compostable paper products and recyclable products available nowadays.

Reducing your water usage is also important in reducing your carbon footprint. Make sure that faucets do not leak or are not left on by accident. Install a water/energy efficient dishwashing machine if possible, and do not use the dishwashing machine when there is not a full load to wash. Cooking equipment can be turned on only when in use. Many food service operators come to work in the morning and turn on all of the equipment, when in reality, they may not need it until many hours later.

Offering meatless, vegetarian or vegan options reduces your carbon footprint because animal production is very costly in terms of use of natural resources. I've heard a related joke that has some truth to it: "A vegetarian driving a Hummer has less carbon footprint than a meat eater driving a Prius." Although I do not have the data to back this up, I know that factory animal or industrial production consumes mass quantities of fossil fuel and contributes mass amounts of methane gas to the atmosphere.

Area of Focus #5: Increase Stewardship Applied to Living Things

This section deals with being kind because kind, thoughtful treatment of people and animals goes along with a culture and system of sustainability.

It is difficult to know what the true cost is in terms of human suffering in the industry of our food production. The American meatpacking industry has been cited as an alleged abuser of its work force. In 1906, Upton Sinclair wrote about this in his book, *The Jungle*. In your foodservice program, you can reduce some of the mystery by meeting your producers and having relationships with all levels of local distribution. Farm visits, as I described earlier, are the best way to know who is growing your food and in what conditions they work. Most of the farmers I have met, from my local farmer friends, Barry and Peggy, to a cranberry grower I met last week, are hard-working, kind folks who care about their workers. Most of them work side-by-side with their employees, but this kind of treatment is not always the case.

Some food service workers work in less than comfortable conditions for low wages and little or no benefits. Personally, I have been lucky in my career to have worked for individuals and companies that have been very fair to me. Kindness to your employees and a coaching/counseling atmosphere create an environment where more care is given. When treated well, employees, and even guests and customers, are more pleasant and your workers will be more productive.

When possible, purchase meat and other protein products that were produced in humane ways. Milk products, yogurt and eggs are non-meat, animal protein products that I buy regularly from farms that treat their animals thoughtfully. I have found that ground turkey, chicken thighs and even quail eggs can be purchased for reasonable prices from farm direct distributors in my area. Often, operators of food service programs feel that they cannot afford sustainably raised meat products in their institution. My advice on this subject is that you should shoot high, and do the best you can, and then accept that there is room for improvement. Michelangelo wisely wrote, "The greater danger for most of us lies not in setting our aim too high and falling short; but in setting our aim too low, and achieving our mark."

Marine animals are affected by our farming practices as well. Realize that the use of chemicals in factory farming may have caused problems with run-off into waterways and has created large "dead zones" in the Gulf of Mexico and the Chesapeake Bay. Scientists and others are acting to reverse this on all levels of the agriculture industry. They are involved in nutrient management activities on a national level. Bees, birds and beneficial bugs can be adversely affected by chemical use. These creatures benefit and thrive when fewer harsh chemicals are deployed on our crops. Small family farms have many reasons not to use large quantities of poisonous chemicals. They want to protect their health and the health of their families and neighbors. They care about clean water sources for their crops, animals and themselves. In addition, chemicals are expensive and add to the cost of their operation.

Area of Focus #6: Create Political Change

You create political change when you buy organic, farm direct or otherwise sustainably produced goods because you are "voting for change with your wallet." Institutions purchase and consume larger quantities of goods than individuals; therefore, when you purchase farm direct products for your institution, you are providing an even larger "vote."

There are many organizations, groups and projects that can get you engaged and educate you further in the political aspects of the farm to school movement. Farm Aid, Earth Day and Food Day are some of the yearly events in which I have been involved. Also, there are national groups, like the Farm School Network, that can inspire and educate. By supporting these groups and events, you are making a political statement for sustainable agriculture and farm to table food.

Area of Focus #7: Support Global Sustainable Agriculture

Supporting global sustainable agriculture adds to your program in several ways. For example, it is a fact that the climate in the northeast United States is not favorable for growing foods like coffee, tea, peppercorns, bananas, chocolate, olives and sugar cane, but in some cases, there are local sustainably grown substitutes. Cane sugar can be replaced with maple products or honey. Spices like black pepper can be replaced with preserved or fresh chilies. Tea can be brewed from dried herbs and other plants, although for me, it's not the same without the caffeine that is in actual tea.

Chocolate, bananas and coffee are not replaceable in my opinion. Most institutions run on coffee. Fair trade, organic, rain forest safe, shade tree grown are some of the key words and phrases that can lead you to sustainable global products. In the case of coffee, I have made friends with some local roasters who have visited the coffee farms around the world and have vetted them for me. One Village Coffee in Montgomery County, PA is the company I prefer.

Crop of hydroponic lettuce at Butter Valley Farm

Global trade is a tricky business, because it is often difficult to know how the goods you are buying were really produced. Locally produced products and global products can be labeled in similar ways. The larger food industry companies want us to be confused in some cases so they can charge more for their product without doing anything different. By labeling it differently, they can call a product "sustainably produced" or "farmer grown" without really defining the meaning of the words. This area of focus is another example of the balance that is inherent in doing a farm to table project. On one hand, you can look for labeled global food items that have the key words and purchase those items; on the other hand, you are not supporting local agriculture by doing so. I have found that one can balance these things and realize that you can "do what you can." To be successful as a business, you must strike a balance. Over time, this balance will change, and you must be prepared to change with it.

Area of Focus #8: Offer People Nutritious Food

Wanting to feed people nutritious food is human nature. If you are working toward a more sustainable food source system, nutrition goes hand-in-hand. Farm direct, sustainably produced goods are inherently more nutritious than highly processed, chemical laden foods.

Educate yourself and your staff about nutrition. I have read that we are seeing breakthrough medical findings everyday about nutrition. Perhaps there is truth to the theory that nutrition is a fairly new medical science compared to, for example, medical surgery, which has been studied clinically for hundreds of years. The detailed chemical processes that take place when food is consumed are very complex. Take, for example, the simple act of eating an apple. There are many chemical compounds, vitamins and other nutrients in an apple. The question is how they all interact and in what ways do we benefit from the natural balance of nutrients in the apple? Perhaps the first people who studied nutrition were shamans, witch doctors and other so-called scientists touting healing potions or remedies. I am sure ancient civilizations, from the Chinese to the Aztecs and Incas, used foods and herbs for healing.

Learn to speak about nutrition. Americans generally eat what is referred to as the Western diet. I tend to be very general when giving advice or speaking about nutrition. I feel strongly that it is generally healthy for everyone who eats the Western diet to learn to eat more fruits, veggies and whole grains, to drink more water, and to cook foods from scratch. Eat less meat in general and eat less fats, refined sugars and salt. I am not comfortable quoting statistics like the amounts of each nutrient a person should have per day. Some experts feel there is a crisis in America regarding obesity, high blood pressure, high cholesterol and heart disease and that the Western diet, which is high in fats, sugars and salts contributes to that.

Open your program to serve nutritious foods to as many people as possible. When business dictates, make prices on healthier foods lower and non-nutritious foods higher. This will offset some costs of the more expensive "healthier products." I have joked that selling chicken fingers pays for some of our local organic products.

Donate all useable food-safe goods to the needy when possible. Plan ahead, and possibly donate leftovers and highly perishable products before your institution closes for the holidays and term breaks. Get involved with local organizations that do service in this area. In

Philadelphia, Philabundance, Food Trust and Fair Food are examples.

Any group can make a plan to pay for and serve good local food. If your institution is getting government subsidized goods or is a prestigious private school, you can afford local food. My good friend, Jessica Borkosky, runs a food service program at a public/charter school, called Leap Academy in Camden, New Jersey, and she has brought a wonderful F2S program to the folks there. All school students should have access to nutritious, sustainably-produced food.

Area of Focus #9: Advocate for Environmental Stewardship

In all areas of your sustainability program, you should advocate for environmental stewardship. This is the key focus point and should be happening on many levels within your organization. From the time the seed is selected to the point that we ingest the meal, there are many opportunities to support environmental stewardship.

Weave all these items together and you will be in a good position to be a green entity. Take it to the next level in your institution. There will be plateaus on your green journey, but just remember: "Life is a journey, not a destination."

Chapter 5: Steps to Bring Farm to Table to Your Environment

There are five logical steps for implementing a farm to table program in your institution:
1. Evaluate the food service program and the school.
2. Start small and plan for the future.
3. Get through the first year.
4. Expand your scope.
5. Take it to the next level because you never know what the future has in store.

Step 1: Evaluate the Food Service Program and the School

The first step is to evaluate the situation. There are many directions you can go in when it comes to bringing F2T to your institution. What is the financial and contractual situation? Can revenues be increased? Can food costs or labor costs be reduced in order to open up funds for the project? What is the baseline from which you can judge customer/client satisfaction? A pre-project survey of your client base is very helpful. Include questions that ask about plated food quality, service and quality of ingredients. Start with general questions and then get more specific about sustainability.

Look at what you currently use and think about what products you could upgrade. You may find that there are some easy substitutions when goods are in season. There are many value added or lightly processed local sustainable products that are available year round and are very consistent in price and quality. Each institution is different and the products you choose to replace and the order in which you replace them should be deemed by the business. I have found at the three institutions where I have implemented farm to table projects that I have been able to buy many varied items that are available year round. Look at your goods and replace as much as possible. Everyone wants quality food at the right price.

Evaluate the people you work with at the institution. Try to figure out whom you can partner with and who will be your advocate for farm to table. You will most likely find folks who grow a vegetable garden at home, visit farm stands and markets and have agriculture in their family history. Making contact and gaining their support is a good start. If there are people who are very passionate about farm to table, they will support you even more.

It is also important to find the folks who will throw roadblocks into the project. Customers may perceive farm direct food as being more costly. Food service workers may view the change as more work. Upper management may need convincing that the program is valuable and you may have some resistance from suppliers. If you can identify some of the people who want to promote sustainability, they can help you move the program forward.

Another great way to evaluate the current food service program is to "get out there," ask questions, listen to people and start conversations. Be available electronically as well. Some people may not be comfortable approaching you in person, so be sure that your email is accessible. A strong web presence through a website or social media could be helpful.

Step 2: Start Small and Plan for the Future

The second step is to start small and plan for the future. This is where you make your first move. You need to get started buying some local goods. Start small with easy to replace goods. Plan the project as you do this step. Do not wait to start buying until after your complete program plan is written. This probably is the opposite approach to every project you have undertaken in the past. It may seem like a "seat of your pants" way of starting the program, but I strongly suggest this approach for starting this kind of program. You will benefit from immediate results and you will quickly find out where folks stand on the issue. You need time to reach out to suppliers and work out delivery schedules, payment plans and storage. You will have to write menus that feature these goods and work out pricing. Many schools have meal plans that you can plan to use some of these goods for.

A marketing system with the goal of educating your clients and staff should be considered. Posters and signs explaining which farms the products come from and where those farms are located is always helpful. You need to let people know what you are doing. Identify the components in prepared dishes that are from local producers. It is critical to start small, take the first step and plan for the future. Remember, Rome was not built in a day.

Some items that have worked for me as first purchases include apples, honey, eggs and potatoes. These goods are available farm to table in my region nearly year round and they are easily stored for use and are very versatile. I have worked with local apples and growers extensively at all of the locations where I instituted a farm to table program.

One tip for using all you buy is to have a plan to sell the "dinged up" or bruised produce in several dishes. Baked apples, applesauce, apple pie, apple stuffing, and apple salads are all great uses for less than perfect apples. Apple cider is available in fall, winter and into the spring in my area, and can be sold by the pint with very little effort.

Potatoes have many uses and can easily be incorporated in any menu. Chefs and cooks may benefit from lots of education and training on how to work with these products in the raw farm direct state. Many institutions rely on produce that is already peeled and possibly cut up, and it is fine to balance out your usage of raw, unprocessed farm direct ingredients with produce in this state.

Honey, for your hot tea program and cooking will most likely cost a little more and should be promoted when purchased. There are many benefits from using local honey. Studies recently have suggested that there may be health benefits relating to allergies that local honey can provide.

Local farm fresh eggs are typically a little more expensive than eggs that are from industrially raised chickens. I do not currently use local eggs exclusively at my account, but I always feature them and keep them in stock for use. It can be a balance depending on the egg consumption, selling price, and production at your facility. A case of farm fresh eggs can go a long way when marketed, portioned, and cooked properly.

Farm direct deliveries are a great way to start out. If you can arrange to have a local orchard deliver the apples directly, that is the best-case scenario. In Pennsylvania, you can currently reach out to Common Market in Philadelphia or Lancaster Farm Fresh Co-op (LFFC) in Lancaster. In New York, you can reach out to Grow NYC, in New Jersey Zone 7. In Delaware, Fifer Orchard and TATurkey will deliver directly to your school, and the Delaware Department of Agriculture can help you find farmers. Common Market and LFFC both deliver to several states and are fantastic resources in our area. There is also a new *USDA know your farmer, know your food compass* that can guide you to local producers as well.

Encourage your employees and supervisors to get excited about your farm to table program. Be excited when deliveries come in. Sample goods and look up information on items you start buying. Teach them a little at a time. Do not go "over the top" all at once or you could overwhelm your staff and set the wrong tone for the project. Your staff is your most important asset. Involve them, treat them kindly and encourage them to succeed.

Please feel strong and comfortable with the outcome of the first step. You must be encouraged by simply knowing that you are doing the right thing and that in the end, it is good for everyone involved. Expect a return on your initial investment of time and resources to be humble. If you can successfully take the first step and buy and sell some local products while meeting your previously established financial goals without having any negative impact, you are doing fine. I do not expect any negative impact from starting a farm to table program, but one must be prepared. The program is designed to be a marathon, not a sprint; take each step as a small victory in a long race. If you need at anytime during the "race" to back off a particular segment of the program, look at it like General Douglas MacArthur, who said, "We are not retreating – we are advancing in a different direction." Advancing in a different direction may keep the flow of the project positive. You will have lots of tasks and sub-projects going at the same time, and focusing on the areas that are succeeding and redirecting areas that are not will keep the whole program stronger.

Check production, sample dishes and raw product (produce), and work with your cooks and chefs on recipe development, flavor profiles, and dish design. As the leader of the project, you have to show interest and excitement toward the products even if you personally dislike the taste or texture. Recently, I purchased a produce item called bitter melon and no amount of cooking and preparing could make it taste good to me and everyone else that had it. I was still excited and passionate about trying it and in the end, the case of bitter melon that I had purchased worked as an educational and marketing purchase. I do not recommend buying bitter melon at your account unless you have a very specific customer base or want to do an educational/marketing sub-project. Whatever you purchase, make sure it gets used, eaten and sold. Check on the production of the goods often and continuously.

Throughout the project, be mindful of the financial picture. Check costs, selling prices and revenue often. During the first step of buying some initial products and planning the bigger picture, you can use the preliminary financial results to gauge some future results. If you find that you are getting better numbers by using one farm direct product or another, maximize the use of it in your future plans. The same theory applies if the products are not working for you financially or educationally – simply discontinue their use. Once you have started using a product like local honey, in which the return is not going to be as measurable as other products because it is a condiment or ingredient, you must maximize the marketing/educational aspects of it. Try not to stop offering it just because the financial return is not positive. Be patient and look at the big picture.

Evaluate customer satisfaction while you are going through all phases of the project. Listen to your customers; they will have feedback about the goods you are purchasing. In some cases, your consumers may be familiar with some of the local farms you are using. Keep your message on a positive note even if the feedback is sometimes not as positive as you would like. It is hard not to defend your decisions or ideas, but being defensive is not positive and you must learn to" build a bridge and get over it."

Make the first move as soon as possible; do it while you are reading this book, or right after. Every journey starts with one step. Like the old Nike ad said, "Just do it."

Step 3: Get Through the First Year

The third step is to get through your first year successfully. To quote a Robert Hunter lyric, "The first days are the hardest days, don't you worry anymore." If you think of the project that way, consider that the first year comprises "the first days." Within the time span of one year, you will be able to work through many of the challenges involved with a farm to institution program. The hardest days of year one may be simple problems with simple solutions.

Seasons change and each one has its offerings. During your first year, you will get full exposure to each season. Write your menu and make dishes with foods in season whenever possible. Promote the seasonal changes with posters, emails, and flyers, on menus and through social media. Farmers are working hard to stretch the seasons in many areas. Winter and early spring can be most challenging in the Northeast. During those seasons, I feature root vegetables, mushrooms, eggs, yogurt, turkey products, potatoes and apples. Mushrooms in my area are local and plentiful year round. We live very near Kennett Square, a huge mushroom growing area.

Always keep in mind the basic food cost principals. Know the cost of the product, the portion size, how many portions you get from one bulk unit, and what the selling price is. If you have this information, you can calculate your food cost. School foodservice operations have many different financial structures. You may have a food cost goal anywhere in a range of 30% to 60%. Private, charter and public schools can make a farm to table program work, but it takes time to develop and upgrade a large percentage of your goods. Over the course of a year, you could hope to replace or introduce 30 or more items. If you consider the different varieties of some produce lines that are now available, like squash, apples, kale, cabbages, potatoes, sweet potatoes, greens, eggplants, peppers and tomatoes when in season, you could have hundreds of choices. I have not counted, but at PCOM, I have introduced perhaps 30 or more in six months. I began running the food services there in the late summer when many products were in season and prices are often lower because of large supplies. You could do that at your location in the same amount of months if your situation is favorable and you are in an area where these items are grown and distribution systems are established.

Products that I would suggest looking for next would include local dairy products. Merrymead Farms in Lansdale delivers to my area and they have award-winning milk products. Local turkey products that I have had success with include drumsticks, boneless skinless thighs, whole turkeys, sausage, ground white meat and burgers. I have bought products from TA Turkey farm in Wyoming, Delaware, and the farm delivers it directly. I also use a farm in Tamaqua, PA, named Koch Turkey Farm. They offer "certified humanely raised" turkey. Both these farms have excellent products and I have met some of the owners and workers who are family farmers that are huge supporters of the farm to table movement. Many pork products can be acquired and used, including bacon, sausage and smoked ham hocks. Locally, sustainably-grown meat items are more costly in most cases. So, for items like the pork cuts I have listed, I feature them as flavorings. I recently bought and served razorback and barbed wire boar at my account from a local farm. We made chili and a small amount of protein went a long way. I think the cost was around $35 for the boar. I have used whole chickens on occasion, and have bought local cheeses for special occasions. I attended a seminar/cheese tasting recently where I learned that several old-style, European cheese makers have relocated to Pennsylvania and the surrounding areas. They are producing exceptional cheese that is on the expensive side but tastes great and is appropriate for special occasions. Beef items can be twice the cost compared to commercial beef. If you can command a higher price, I recommend it. Local bison is available year round. I have used ground, cubed and bison heart recently. With bison and other expensive meats, you can stretch your protein dollars by making chili, lasagna, stew or any other dish that can have veggies incorporated into it. In addition, there are many vegetables, herbs and greens available seasonally. Try the basics first, and then move onto the more interesting exotic-type goods.

It is helpful to repeat menu dishes regularly the first year. This will increase popularity and allow your staff to create a more consistent recipe. Side dishes, pizzas, soups, breakfast items and composed salads are popular and work well with farm to table goods. Mashed potatoes, baked apples, and cream of broccoli soup are three quick examples of great, hot dishes, when in season. Tomato, fresh mozzarella and basil (salad caprice) work well as a composed salad, and is another favorite of mine.

Since food is perishable, there will be times when items won't get used quickly enough or completely. If you are committed to a farm to school program and buy many and various items, there will be times when there will be shrinkage of stock in the form of spoilage. Use these occasions as learning opportunities and move on. Be careful when receiving goods into your establishment. Make sure goods are up to your standards and are high quality when they arrive. If you are buying "#2" quality or "utility" quality produce, you should expect some damage. Speak to your suppliers about their definition of these terms when ordering these goods. I have heard different definitions of what a #2 quality product should look like. My recommendation would be to look at each case, farmer and product individually. Due to past experience, I know what a case of canning tomatoes should look like and cost for example, and there are a lot of uses for juicy ripe canning tomatoes.

Evaluate the financial impact of your F2S program at every point you can. Most institutions do a complete inventory with a profit and loss statement at the end of each month. Compare the results to the same month the previous year. Always keep in mind that there is a financially incalculable gain in the form of marketing and customer satisfaction that should be considered as a positive outcome of a successful program. Customers generally do not care if a food service operation is making money. They care that they are getting quality food and great service at a good price. I like to say, "I work to offer the right food at the right price." This does not mean that I want to lose money or "make a killing." Every location should have a budget and food and labor cost percentages that they strive for. Each location needs to determine what their costs should be. Some food service programs receive subsidies in order to keep prices low, to offer certain hours of business or to get better products for their faculty and students. Administrators and management team leaders may ask themselves what the value is in keeping their employees or students healthy and happy, and how a F2S program can help with that.

A one-year evaluation in writing is a good idea. Certainly, a report on the numbers from your monthly statements, as previously discussed, is in order. A full year financial and customer satisfaction evaluation will be very telling. This will force you to change and grow. If everyone is generally happy with the changes, look more closely at the details, because complacency will lead to negative results down the road. I would expect that if you follow my formula, you should have a successful year-end result. If there are too many negatives, look at the bigger picture and understand the dynamics of your situation. Complex personnel training or systems issues could lead to a lot of small problems. If you adjust during the first year process, only tweaking will be necessary to improve your program in the following years. If you work for a contract feeding company, you are keeping your customer base and clients happy, and you are meeting your financial goals for your company, then you are doing things right.

Step 4: Expand Your Scope

Step four is to expand your scope. You have completed your first year with steps two and three, you have bought lots of goods by now, and your customer base is established. Now, you can branch out and support your program by adding "value added" functions, menus, promotions and events. After some time, you may develop statewide, national and even international contacts.

Make more local contacts with like-minded people. Expand your group of farm to table partners. There are many groups and individuals that are involved in farm to table around the country. If you are near a metropolitan area that has easy access to farm direct products, finding more like-minded people in the industry will perhaps be easier. Some universities are very involved in agriculture education and research. The University of Delaware and Penn State in my area have been very helpful and are on the cutting edge of agriculture technology. In the Philadelphia region, there are local chapters of groups like Slow Food, PASA, and Fair Food that you can connect with directly. Learn what they are doing and take what you can back to your institution.

Government groups like USDA and the Department of Agriculture at the state level can be very helpful. Reach out to these entities and invite them to join you in the endeavor. In Delaware, Secretary of Agriculture, Ed Kee, has been a great contact and partner with Sanford School, where I worked. He also worked with me to promote and educate people about farm to table. Making connections in your area may be easier or more difficult depending on the size of your state and how much agriculture business your state does. Keep in mind that "local" does not mean only your state. The USDA is a great resource nationally. You may have to travel to make USDA connections, but the Internet can be a very useful tool for this as well. I have been to several USDA-hosted lectures and they are very helpful.

Reach out to national groups like the National Farm to School Network. In the educational setting, this group is a tremendous leader. When we are feeding kids and young adults, there is a greater focus on nutrition and healthy eating in general. Reach out to any national group you can find.

Working on step four, you will get your chance to broaden your programs and expand your scope. You may get involved in hosting a farm stand or farm market, starting garden or orchard projects, organizing farm visits or hosting farm to table cooking demonstrations. You may get involved in producing value-added products and preserving products for the future. Canning, freezing, dehydrating and curing are all valuable exercises that will stretch the seasons. Start small, maybe make some hot pepper jelly or basil pesto and freeze it in small containers. If you have the production facility, the freezer space and the manpower, you can buy products at their peak of the harvest when they are inexpensive and process them and use them all year. Canning for dry storage is considerably more complicated but would be a wonderful project. Check with your local health department to be sure that you are compliant.

Step 5: Take it to the Next Level

Now that you have completed steps one through four, you may consider step five. This is where I leave it to you to enter the unknown future. Dream big and use your imagination. We will take the farm to table movement and turn it into a powerful industry. That will strengthen the family farms in America, and make our world a more environmentally sustainable place. The purchasing power of groups at institutions can have tremendous impact on the food service industry, and you can be a big part of that.

Conclusion

I could never have envisioned that my journey from childhood to the present would bring me to the forefront of a movement that is growing in popularity and is being utilized in a number of settings. I hope this book gives you the information you need to take the first steps to incorporate farm to school activities into your educational setting. I have shared with you what I have learned in this journey and I would love to hear about your journey in the future.

As a thank you for purchasing my book, I would like to offer you a one-hour consultation to get you started. Please visit my website at chefbuddcohen.com for the latest updates. I may be reached at chefdad007@gmail.com.

Quick Reference Guide for Farm to Table Information Nationally and Locally:

The USDA – Know your farmer, know your food compass: http://www.usda.gov/http://www.usda.gov/

The National Farm to School Network: http://www.farmtoschool.org/http://www.farmtoschool.org/

Farm Aid: http://www.farmaid.org/http://www.farmaid.org/

Common Market: http://commonmarketphila.org/http://commonmarketphila.org/

Lancaster Farm Fresh Co-Op: http://www.lancasterfarmfresh.com/http://www.lancasterfarmfresh.com/

Phoenixville Farmers Market: http://www.phoenixvillefarmersmarket.org/http://www.phoenixvillefarmersmarket.org/

Leesport Farmers Market: http://www.leesportmarket.com/

Acknowledgements

This book would not have been possible without the help of many people, and I would like to single out just a few:

Thank you, Judy Weintraub, for inspiring me to write a book on this subject.

To Timmy Lynch, for your support over the years and friendship and your willingness to write a fantastic Foreword. Many thanks!

Special thanks to my cousin, Helene Cohen-Bludman, a writer and blogger at booksiswonderful.com for reading each draft and making suggestions along the way.

Thank you to Cheryl Carmel, for her beautiful picture.

To the CulinArt group, I am grateful for your encouragement to pursue this project with your enthusiastic endorsement.

My passion for farm to table would not exist if it were not for the many farmers who have welcomed me into their world.

Finally, I would like to thank my wife, Stacey, and my children, Alex and Abby, for making everything worthwhile.

About the Author

Chef Budd Cohen has been on the cutting edge of the farm to school movement through his experience in educational food service, his insatiable curiosity about local food production and his love of tasty food.

He is currently the Food Service Director at Philadelphia College of Osteopathic Medicine and he consults with organizations that are interested in exploring the farm to table experience. He lives in Audubon, PA with his wife and two children.

Chef Cohen can be reached by email to chefdad007@msn.com. For more information, visit his website at www.chefbuddcohen.com.

Printed in the USA
CPSIA information can be obtained
at www.ICGtesting.com
CBHW080514231024
16226CB00032B/105